Aborigines of Australia

The Aborigines have lived in Australia for thousands of years. They probably originated in Southeast Asia and migrated across land that is now submerged. They evolved a way of life suited to their country, living by gathering food and hunting. There were many different tribes throughout Australia, living on their tribal lands until the Europeans arrived in the 1780s. Confrontations with the settlers, tribal wars and disease decimated the population. By the 1950s their numbers had greatly diminished, but they are now increasing once more. The author, Robyn Holder, is an Australian who has studied Aboriginal history and culture, and now works with a number of international groups involved with Aboriginal affairs. She vividly describes the history and rich mythological traditions of the Aboriginal peoples, and explains their aims and aspirations in present-day Australia.

Original Peoples

ABORIGINES
OF AUSTRALIA

Robyn Holder

Rourke Publications, Inc.
Vero Beach, FL 32964

Original Peoples

Eskimos — The Inuit of the Arctic
Aborigines of Australia
Plains Indians of North America
South Pacific Islanders
Indians of the Andes
Zulus of Southern Africa

First published in the
United States in 1987 by
Rourke Publications, Inc.
Vero Beach, FL 32964

Library of Congress Cataloging-in-Publication Data

Holder, Robyn.
    Aborigines of Australia.

    (Original peoples)
    Bibliography: p.
    Includes index.
    Summary: Surveys the history, tribal groups,
social life, customs, and gradual assimilation of the
Australian aborigines and discusses their struggle
to retain their racial identity while fighting for
their rights..
    1. Australian aborigines — Juvenile literature.
[1. Australian aborigines] I. Title. II. Series.
GN665.H65 1987   994'004991   87-4322
ISBN 0-086625-262-2

Photoset by Direct Image Photosetting
Printed in Italy by G. Canale & C.S.p.A., Turin

Contents

Introduction 6

Chapter 1 The Dreamtime

How the World Was Made 8

The Living Past 10

Chapter 2 The Aboriginal People

From the Land Itself 12

The Many Tribes 14

"My Country" 16

Chapter 3 Living on the Land

Hunting and Gathering 18

Family and Kin 20

Learning 22

Becoming Adults 24

Chapter 4 The British Invasion

Convicts and Soldiers 26

War and Disease 28

Missionaries 30

Protection 32

Chapter 5 The Dispossessed

Assimilation 34

Fringe-dwellers 36

Racism 37

The Tent Embassy 38

Chapter 6 Land Rights Now!

Self-determination 40

People vs. Profit 42

"Listen to Us!" 44

Glossary 46

Glossary of Pitjantjatjara Words 47

Books to Read 47

Index 48

Introduction

A common picture of Aboriginal life before the British colonization of Australia is of a people wandering through arid deserts in a constant search for food and water. The reality was a quite different story. The whole of Australia was a web of tribal territories.

This early engraving shows an Aboriginal family carrying the few tools and weapons needed for their way of life.

Aboriginal people were semi-nomadic, which means they moved from camp site to camp site. They made weapons and implements that suited their lifestyle perfectly. In any season within their territory they knew where to find food and water. By keeping the Laws of the Dreamtime (Laws given them by the Ancestral Beings many thousands of years ago) there was no reason to fear the country nor to worry about the future. Theirs was a balanced life.

The Aboriginal religion, the

Dreaming, explains how the landscape, the animals, plants and people were created. It is a complete worldview, taking in all that is known and all that is understood. The Dreamtime is kept alive through ceremony, song and learning. It gives Aborigines a knowledge of the past, stability in the present and security for the future.

Many Aboriginal people have kept their religion of the Dreamtime, or have returned to it. More are finding the strength and determination to continue the old way of life in a changed world. It is remarkable that Aboriginal culture and ways of life are still so strong after almost 200 years of abuse and misunderstanding on the part of white people.

Aboriginal people recognize a need to adapt to the new society that surrounds them in Australia today. They also want the white people to learn from them, and to recognize their different way of life. This book is an introduction to Aboriginal culture and history. It explains the demands Aborigines are making today for their land, for justice and for equality.

Although there are many Aboriginal languages, this book uses only one, that of the *Pitjantjatjara* tribe.

A representation of Aboriginal tribal territories before the British invasion.

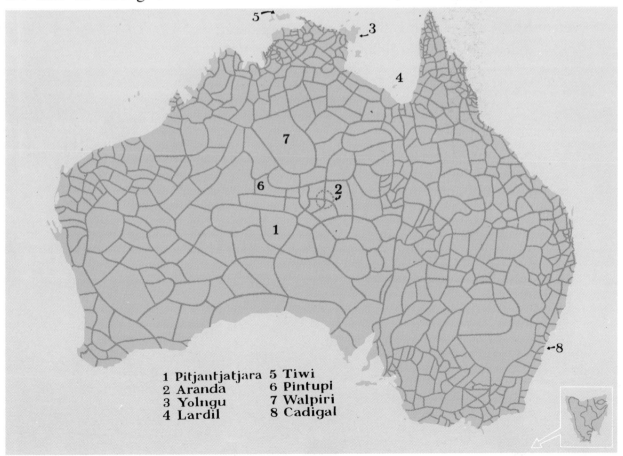

1 Pitjantjatjara 5 Tiwi
2 Aranda 6 Pintupi
3 Yolngu 7 Walpiri
4 Lardil 8 Cadigal

Chapter 1 **The Dreamtime**

How the World Was Made

Right at the very beginning of the world there was no sun. The land was flat, dark, cold and barren. Nothing lived and nothing moved. But under the ground the Ancestral Beings were sleeping. Stretching and yawning, they broke out from their sleeping places. They saw that there was no light and so created the sun. Its rays warmed the earth.

Some of the Ancestors were men and women and others were like animals, birds and plants. Some were even in the form of rain, clouds and stars. Whatever their shape, the Ancestors behaved just like humans. They moved around the land. They traveled great distances, hunted and fought. The paths they took are called Dreaming Tracks. These tracks are very important because they link the whole land and the people together.

Sometimes the Ancestors actually made the land, but mostly they shaped what was already there. They made the mountains, the rivers, the trees, the waterholes, the plains and sand hills. They made all animals and

Kundaagi, *the red plains kangaroo, is an Ancestor of many Aboriginal people.*

plants and they made people. To these people the Ancestors entrusted the care of the land and of all living things on it.

Worn out from their work, they finally sank back into the earth. Some changed into rocks or trees or even into small islands. All these places the Ancestors passed over or stopped at are very special to Aborigines. The Ancestors left signs of their presence and power. These are holy places called sacred sites. The Aborigines are their descendants, and they call the time in which the Ancestors moved on the earth, the Dreamtime.

Any rock or natural formation could be the body of an Ancestor, or a sacred site.

Toby Naninga and Jack Nangalay are the traditional owners of Uluru (Ayers Rock). *Many Dreaming Tracks intersect here.*

The Living Past

To the Aboriginal people the Dream-time is the time of Creation. In the *Pitjantjatjara* language they call it *Tjukurpa*. A great many legends go to make up the Dreamtime.

Each person was born with their own Dreaming or totem. For example, Honey Ant Dreaming *(tjala)* would relate a boy or girl to the honey ant. The *tjala* would belong to a certain place where it had resided ever since its Ancestor had left it there in the Dreamtime. The person with the Honey Ant Dreaming is considered to be a direct descendant of that particular Ancestor. They could not eat or harm the honey ant.

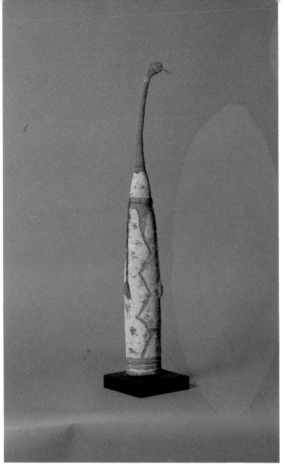

Ceremonies, like this one in Arnhem land, re-enact the times of the Ancestral Beings.

Above *The totem of the long-necked, fish-eating bird, called* Niliwginei.

The Dreaming place of the honey ant is *milmilpa,* which means sacred.

The Dreamtime is the ever present link between Aboriginal people, nature and the spiritual world. If a person lost that link, he or she lost their soul, their Dreaming. This happened to many Aborigines when the British invaded their country and took their land, the land of their Dreaming.

But the spirit of the Ancestors is always present in the land, or the *manta,* and in the people, the *anangu.* The Ancestors gave the people laws about how to live together and how to live from the land without harming it. This is the "straight and true way," the Laws of *Tjukurpa.*

When a person performs a particular ceremony according to the Law, the Dreamtime lives again. The past is dramatically brought alive. The ceremony for the person with the Honey Ant Dreaming recreates the making of the honey ant by its Ancestor. The person becomes the honey ant and the Ancestor. Their link from Ancestor to place of birth is strengthened. For Aboriginal people, the Dreamtime and its Laws are as true today as when the Ancestors first walked the earth. Keeping the land means keeping the soil, the Dreaming.

Rock paintings are often thousands of years old. They record Aboriginal history and religion.

Chapter 2 **The Aboriginal People**

From the Land Itself

Many Aboriginal people believe that they were created by the Ancestors from the land itself. They say that they have always been in Australia from the very beginning.

The *Aranda* tribe in central Australia say that two brothers, the *Numbakulla,* lived in the western sky. The *Numbakulla* looked down and saw spirit people, the *Inapatua,* crouched under low boulders on the shores of the salt lakes. The *Inapatua* could not move, see or hear. Coming down to earth with their stone knives, the *Numbakulla* carved from the rock the arms and legs of the *Inapatua.*

They opened the mouths, eyes, ears and noses of the spirit people. The *Inapatua* could see, hear and smell! They could move! They spread out over the country. They were the first of the *Aranda* tribe.

The people in the north of Western Australia believe that their Ancestors, the *Wandjina,* came from the sea with their families and companions. The *Wandjina* made the first people for that country. All the stories of the Dreamtime explain how Aborigines are descended from their

This sacred burial site uncovered by the wind, is thousands of years old.

Johnnie Bulun and his family with a painting that maps his ancestral country.

Below *Spirit children, left by the Ancestors, often live in waterholes waiting to be born.*

Ancestral Beings.

Anthropologists say that the Aborigines came to Australia over 50,000 years ago. At that time Australia was joined to New Guinea in the north and to Tasmania in the south. The people were able to move over this land bridge into Australia. They occupied the fertile coasts first and then the dry, inland regions. The first Aborigines, the anthropologists say, also traveled great distances by sea from Asia. These people sailed in canoes and rafts, the earliest boats in the world. Both the Aborigines and the anthropologists agree that Aboriginal people have lived in Australia for thousands of years.

The Many Tribes

When white people first came to Australia they called all the original people, "aboriginal." This means people who lived in a place from the earliest known time. Other descriptions are indigenous, native or indian.

The Aborigines actually belonged to different tribes or language groups and called themselves different names. The name is the same as the language they speak. So, the people who speak *Pitjantjatjara* are known as the *Pitjantjatjara*. Other names are *Yolngu*, *Lardil*, *Tiwi*, *Aranda*, *Pintupi*, *Walpiri* and *Cadigal*. There were nearly 500 of these tribes — too many to list here! They spoke over 200 languages and 300 dialects.

Special ceremonies take place when tribes come together to trade and meet relatives.

Bark huts provide shelter and are made quickly whenever a cap is set up.

Each tribal group also has a name for itself meaning "the people." The *Pitjantjatjara* call themselves, *Anangu*. The *Walpiri* call themselves, *Yapa*. People in the southeast part of Australia call themselves *Koories*. Aborigines in the northeast call themselves *Murries*. In the west and south the name is *Nungas*. To speak of the Aborigines as though they were one single group is obviously not accurate.

The tribes were made up of smaller groups called clans or landowning groups. Even smaller groups consisted of extended families. The extended family included the father, one or more wives, and all the children. Grandparents and other older relatives also lived with the family and were looked after by them.

The types of shelter varied from place to place and from season to season. In hot, dry areas people made grass windbreaks to shelter under. In the rainy north, people had huts on stilts. In the colder parts the huts were more substantial and were made of rocks or branches. Some families stayed in one place for six months at a time. Other families moved nearly every week, depending on the availability of food.

15

"My Country"

All the tribes had their own territory or estate, called their *ngura*. This was given to them by the Ancestral Beings and could not be bought or sold, lost or bartered. Within the territories were many sacred sites, the signs left by the Ancestors. It was the duty of the men *(wati)* to look after these sites and to perform the proper ceremonies related to each site. Older women also had such sacred sites to tend and duties to carry out.

Around the coast, in the woodlands and plains of the south and east, and in the rain forests, food and water were plentiful. Here the tribal territories were small. Over 90 percent of the Aboriginal people once lived in these areas. The majority of white Australians now live there. The rest of the Aboriginal people lived in the rocky and sandy deserts of the interior. Their territories were often thousands of square miles in extent. Each tribe had enough territory to hunt and gather sufficient food for everyone in it.

Although there were no fences or borders dividing up the land, Aborigines knew exactly where their country began and ended. Children *(tjitjitjuta)* learned from an early age what their personal Dreaming place was and what their tribal country was to mean to them. They were told that the

This Pitjantjatjara *group live securely on their own country in central Australia.*

Nagara people (on the right) await permission to approach their neighbors' camp and to enter their country.

legends, songs and arts of the Dreamtime were like title deeds. They would have their own deeds to their own Dreaming (for example, the Honey Ant).

The songs described the journeys of the Ancestors and of the tracks they made. They explained where to hunt and gather and in what season. Songs were like maps. A knowledgeable person might know an area, even if he or she had never been there, simply because the song for that country described it.

Chapter 3 **Living on the Land**

Hunting and Gathering

Australia is a very large country. The climate and environment differ from area to area. The area where a tribe lived would influence how they lived.

Desert people, like the *Pitjantjat-jara*, would move from camp to camp quite often. The camps and the paths between them were made by the Ancestors in the Dreamtime. The lives of the tribes were very closely tied to nature. They did not dig or plant or harvest. They conserved and nurtured the environment so that there would always be food and water *(kapi)* available.

Women gathered the bulk of the family's food. Everyone relied on their work. Mothers, aunties and children would all take part in gathering bush tucker. They took with them digging sticks, dillybags and wooden bowls (sometimes called coolamons).

Young boys would go gathering

Some Aborigines practice fire-stick farming, which brings new growth to the land.

too. When they were older they would hunt with the men. The men were excellent hunters. They could follow a kangaroo *(malu)* over rocky ground without losing its tracks. Spears could be thrown a great distance with spear throwers called woomeras. Some tribesmen also used a hunting boomerang. They could kill a bird in flight. Only a few weapons like these were needed. Today, guns and trucks are also used but men still kill only what is necessary to feed the family or clan.

The pattern of life was attuned to the turning of the seasons. The instructions contained in the Dreamtime songs told people where and when to get food and water. Sometimes life was hard but then a tribe that was suffering from drought or hunger would be invited into

This Aboriginal woman has some honey ants (tjala) *gathered in the bush.*

A successful fishing trip at Liverpool River in Arnhem Land.

neighboring territory to share food and water. Aboriginal people were sure of their world, sure of the Dreamtime Law and content in their way of life.

Family and Kin

White society at the time of the invasion of Australia was very different from Aboriginal society. Europeans stress the rights and needs of individuals. Aborigines stress sharing, caring and responsibility toward each other. Personal greed and ambition are frowned on. A most important skill children learn is how to behave toward everyone they may meet.

This skill is part of Aboriginal kinship systems. These systems organize Aboriginal societies in a very ordered way. It is one of the most difficult parts of Aboriginal society for outsiders to understand. Aboriginal children learn just as we do who their aunts and uncles are. But kinship pattern relates them to more people than their immediate family. It relates them to everyone

Many tribes are divided into sections called moieties. *These men are painted with different designs showing their moieties.*

All these children from Jay Creek in the Northern Territory, are related to each other according to kinship rules.

from their grandmother to a neighboring clan member. For example, a boy would call his father's brother, "father," and his father's sister, "aunt." He would call his mother's sister, "mother" and his mother's brother, "uncle." The children of his aunts, uncles, mother's sisters and father's brothers, the boy would call "brother" and "sister." Each relative had a special name called a *skin* name. A child also had his or her own personal name. As soon as a child heard someone's skin name, he or she would know how they were related. So, it would seem as though everyone was a relative!

All this seems complex but it made children feel safe and loved. The *Mowanjum* in northwest Australia say to a boy,

You were not just born for me, you were born for the whole neighborhood. They rejoiced when you were born, oh, you are a real man born to us.

By learning these relationships, a child, or *tjitji*, would know the correct way to behave toward everyone. When the time came to marry, the kinship rules dictated the choice of husband or wife.

21

Learning

All the knowledge about kinship patterns was not written down in books for children. Aborigines did not have a written language. Instead, they had to memorize everything. You could say that they carried their libraries in their heads!

Aborigines have other forms of learning. They can read a rock, bark or body painting as we can read a book. The Dreamtime songs, we

Aranda boys learn bushcraft from an uncle. He is showing them wild honey.

know, are like survival guides and mental maps of the land. All these things — the arts, songs and ceremonies — are the ways in which children learn the history and culture of their people.

While they are young, children lead a carefree and happy life. Games often imitate the activities of older people. Boys in central Australia practice their spear throwing by trying to hit a rolling bar disk. Girls use leaves for a game called *muni-muni*. They use them as puppets, laying them on the ground in patterns. They recall family travels and life around the camp with these leaf-puppets.

The children's learning is not separated from everyday life. They learn by watching and by joining in. *Wuduu* (a *Mowanjum* word meaning "laying of hands") is another way

This Aboriginal woman teaches her children by drawing in the sand.

Children learn dance and ceremony from an early age by joining in with adults.

children learn. Every morning and every night the mother and grandmother warm their hands over the fire. When they touch the child's forehead, that means the lesson of giving; when they touch the eyes, they mean them not to see evil things; touching the mouth means not to use bad language; touching hands means not to steal what didn't belong; and the feet, not to trespass on other people's land. Then they tell the child about sharing. They teach these things for the good of communal life.

23

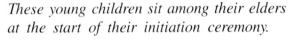

These young children sit among their elders at the start of their initiation ceremony.

Below *Body painting is an important part of the ceremonies of adulthood.*

Becoming Adults

Childhood ends gradually for young girls. Older women perform special, sometimes secret, ceremonies for the young girl. As a young woman she is called *kunka*. By the time she has had two children she is called *minyma*.

The work of gathering food and looking after the children is shared among the women. Much time is taken in singing to and teaching the children. As she grows older, a woman may become a leader in the secret, sacred life of women. She is the bearer and giver of life. A very important part of ritual life was and still is the increase ceremonies. These are held to make sure that rains will fall, that fruit will grow and that animal life is plentiful.

Passing into manhood is a much more abrupt thing for a boy. His training and initiation may take between a month and six months, but it happens all of a sudden. Some tribes say that a boy dies and is born again at this time. Usually he is kept away from women and children during initiation. Many ceremonies are performed. Boys are told the secrets of the Dreamtime religion and Law. They must undergo physical trials.

The time of initiation is the beginning of a life of learning. Stage by stage, men and women are taught about the creation of the world, of people, and of all living creatures. The older a man or woman becomes, the more they are respected for their knowledge. This knowledge is sacred; it is *milmilpa*. It is also an experience of life and how to survive. Aboriginal education is for all people. Learning is a very special part of their lives. Education also means that everyone has a say in the affairs of their clan. There are no chiefs. Each person has to agree to something happening. And any person who breaks the Laws is punished, even today.

In this ritual, women are trying to frighten boys away from the men.

Chapter 4 **The British Invasion**

Convicts and Soldiers

In 1770, Captain James Cook sailed up the east coast of Australia, landing at different places. Captain Cook had been instructed to take possession of strategic points in the country for the King of Great Britain. In doing this he was supposed to gain the consent of the Aborigines. But he asked no one.

British jails at this time contained many prisoners. The growth of industry had drawn thousands of people into overcrowded cities. A small number of aristocrats owned vast amounts of wealth and land in Britain. But the majority of people went hungry and were poor. Some were imprisoned when they stole food to eat and cloth to wear. Life was a struggle to survive and made these people hard. In 1788 the British government began sending shiploads of convicts to Australia so that there would be less prisoners in the jails.

After only a few months in Australia, the British and the Aborigines began fighting each other. The British colony set up there was on the territory of the *Cadigal* tribe. These people became angry when the British abused Aboriginal women and cut down the trees. They were taking too much food, disturbing the land and building cottages on their sacred places. They wanted the white people to leave. The British did these things because they did not know any other way to live and get food.

For the death of one white man, the first ten Aborigines caught were to be killed. In this case the Aborigines got away.

Neither people understood the other.

The *Cadigal* and neighboring tribespeople were horrified by the British. They saw people being flogged with whips, working in chain gangs and hanged with ropes. The Aborigines must have thought the British quite savage at times. But the British colony kept spreading and spreading. Gradually, they began

On January 26, 1788, Governor Phillip raised the Union Jack over Sydney Cove claiming Australia for Britain.

taking more and more land from the tribes. And the tribes fought back.

On June 6, 1835, the only treaty for the purchase of land from Aborigines was made.

War and Disease

The British brought other things besides whips and rum. They brought disease. The sort of sickness Aborigines sometimes had was usually cured with natural medicines. Their diet and way of life kept them healthy. But after 1788, thousands died from the common cold brought to Australia by the British. And thousands more died from smallpox and tuberculosis.

But the real struggle was over land. The British knew very well that all the land was occupied by the Aborigines. Yet they chose to call Australia "waste land." They believed that people should live in towns and farm the land with hoes and plows. Very few could understand how well Aborigines lived from the plants and animals of the land.

Aborigines owned their land because the Dreamtime Ancestors had given it to them. The British thought that the Aborigines merely wandered around. They couldn't see any fences or "Keep Off" signs. So, the fight was also over the ownership of the land. Aborigines fought to keep their tribal country. They killed cattle and sheep. They burned crops. A great many people were killed, both Aboriginal and British.

At times the war was terrible. There were massacres on both sides.

These Aborigines in chains are prisoners of war and were captured in 1906.

Whole tribes were completely wiped out. Over a period of 150 years, nearly 80 percent of the Aboriginal people were killed. The last massacre took place as late as 1928.

Aboriginal people remember with pride the warriors who fought to keep their country. Yagan fought around what is today Perth; Mosquito and a woman named Walyer tried to defend Tasmania; Tuckiar fought in Arnhem Land; Pemulwy in the

This early picture shows the beginning of the struggles between white settlers and Aborigines.

Sydney region; and Dundalli near Brisbane. These are a few of the names among the many who fought and perished.

Aboriginal warriors fought bravely against the invaders and massacres took part on both sides.

Missionaries

The white people held many mistaken ideas about the Aborigines. For example, they thought Aborigines were uncivilized because they did not wear lots of clothes and did not live in houses. They thought the British way of life was superior to any other way in the world. Part of this stemmed from the idea that Christianity was the only true religion, and that it preserved British morals and standards.

Aboriginal religion said that the whole land was sacred. There was no need for churches. All people had their sacred ceremonies, songs and Dreaming. There was no need for priests.

Early missionaries did not understand the ceremonies and Dreamtime religion.

But the British believed that Aborigines had no religion at all. The best thing for the Aborigines, it was commonly thought, was to convert them to Christianity. The Bishop of Adelaide said in 1860:

"I would rather they died as Christians than drag out a miserable existence as heathens.
I believe that the race will disappear either way."

Such an attitude seems very callous to us today. The missionaries tried to keep Aborigines in one place. They tried to make them live the way Europeans do and to worship the Christian God.

These missionaries are teaching Aboriginal children words and music to hymns.

In the twentieth century, missionaries and governments separated mixed-race children from their black mothers. These children were fostered into white families. Or they were sent into homes to work as servants

Christian missionaries tried to divert Aborigines away from their native religion.

and nannies. Often, they received no wage for the work they did. Many mixed-race children were also brought up in the institutions and lost all contact with their families.

The idea of the missionaries and of the government was that these children would grow up to be like white people. This practice was very heartrending for both parents and children. It is remembered with sadness and anger today.

Chapter 5 **The Dispossessed**

Assimilation

Most Europeans now live along the east coast, the inland areas of the south and east, and on the far south-west coast of Australia. These are the most fertile areas where the majority of Aboriginal people used to live. But, over the years, Aborigines were driven from their land. They were dispossessed.

From the beginning of the twentieth century, Aborigines were forced or were drawn into settlements. The government policy was to separate them from the bad influences of white society.

The Second World War brought some changes for Aborigines. Some army camps were set up in places where Aborigines still lived in a largely traditional way. For the soldiers, it was the first time that they had had close contact with Aboriginal people. The army's policy was to employ Aborigines as general workers, cooks and cleaners. They provided decent homes for Aborigines and a decent wage.

The experiences of the army helped to change the attitude of the Australian government. For many years Aborigines had been ignored. From the 1950s, the government introduced a policy called assimilation. Many reserves were closed down in order to force Aborigines into the white society. Australia was to be one nation made up of one people. Aborigines were to

Assimilation cannot work if there are no jobs for these Aboriginal children.

Aboriginals living in cities still take great pride in their cultural identities.

live among whites and go to work regularly. They were to learn the English language, culture and history. Eventually, the government believed, there would be no differences between them and the white Australians.

But this policy did not work. It ignored Aboriginal people's own languages, culture and history. It did not understand the Aboriginal way of life. The uniqueness of Aboriginal society was to be changed. White society was not expected to change.

Many Aborigines make money by selling artifacts.

Fringe-dwellers

The term "fringe-dwellers" means people who live on the edge of society. When Aborigines were pressured into joining white society they had no homes or jobs to go to. Therefore, they had to live in camps on the outskirts of towns. Or they lived in small, overcrowded ghettoes in the cities and in humpies on the cattle stations. They were forced to live on government welfare. They were literally fringe-dwellers.

In many camps there was no running water, electricity or sanitation. Child deaths were over twice the average for white Australians. The bad conditions created skin diseases and respiratory problems. Many children suffered from malnutrition. Years of neglect had meant that there were few facilities for health or education.

However, in the outlying regions, Aborigines retained much of their language, culture and religion. They worked on the cattle stations for rations of meat, tea, sugar and tobacco, and were considered more fortunate.

Because of discrimination, some Aborigines demonstrated in Sydney in 1983.

Aborigines feel happy on their land, but in the cities they often feel "all mixed up."

Racism

Australia is often called the lucky country because of its high standard of living but it has not been lucky for the Aborigines. Although the government had the power to help them, it did very little. The policy of assimilation was not working because many whites did not want to live close to Aborigines. They still held mistaken beliefs about them and wanted to keep themselves apart from them. This was one aspect of

The fringe-dwellers of Alice Springs have no land or homes. The Todd River is the only place they have to live.

racism that meant that Aborigines would not be accepted in to white society.

Aboriginal people are very aware of their separate identity and take great pride in their culture and history. They do not want to lose their identity to become like white people. But they do not want to carry on being victimized simply because they are different.

The Tent Embassy

For many years, some Aboriginal people had protested against discrimination. Their protests, for example, had drawn attention to the conditions and injustice on the reserves in New South Wales.

Some trade unions and others supported the strike of the *Gurindji* people at the Wave Hill cattle station in the Northern Territory. The *Gurindji* had walked off the station in 1968 in protest against low wages. The campaign eventually led to the government policy of a minimum wage for Aboriginal stockmen and women. The cattle station, which the people now own, was on the *Gurindji's* tribal land.

The Land Rights movement wants some land returned to the Aboriginal owners.

A great many Aborigines and white people were involved in campaigning for equal rights for Aborigines. This resulted in a referendum in 1967 that granted citizenship and the right to vote to Aboriginal people. Despite this success, many Aborigines still felt like strangers in their own land. An Aboriginal Tent Embassy was set up in front of Parliament House in Canberra in 1972 to symbolize this feeling. This action brought to the attention of the world the struggle of the Aboriginal people.

In the 1960s, Aborigines in the

center, north and west of Australia had begun to move away from big government settlements and missions where they were "all mixed up" — too many different tribes in one place. They wished to live in smaller clan groups in country camps at the places of their Dreaming. This movement is often called the Outstation or Homelands Movement.

In 1976, the Land Rights Act returned some land to the Aboriginal owners in the Northern Territory.

In 1975 the Australian Prime Minister officially returned land to the Gurindji tribe.

The Act was a limited form of Land Rights because only traditional people could claim land. But it was a beginning. Aboriginal Australians began to hope that at last things might get better.

In 1972 the Aboriginal Tent Embassy made a protest in Canberra against racial discrimination and for Land Rights.

Chapter 6 **Land Rights Now!**

Self-determination

Self-determination means Aboriginal control over their own lives. It means the right to decide how and where they live. And it means the right to determine their own future. The buildup of Aboriginal protest has forced Australian governments into accepting this policy.

Aboriginal Legal Services have been formed to represent Aboriginal people in court and to advise them on legal problems. The services are necessary because too many Aboriginal people are now in jail for minor offenses.

Aboriginal Medical Services have been set up to provide better health care for them. There are also welfare,

The Aboriginal Legal Services provides aid for Aborigines in courts.

housing and education organizations. Most of the organizations are run and staffed by Aborigines. White doctors and lawyers assist with Aboriginal work until the people themselves are trained to take over.

Land Councils exist to claim back

Aborigines have their own radio station and media association.

traditional lands and lands from which Aborigines can earn their own living. Farms and cattle stations are now owned and run by Aborigines. The Councils have come together as the National Federation of Land Councils. The aim of the Land Councils is to achieve real land rights for Aboriginal people. They want full ownership of Aboriginal land and the right to say who may enter their territory.

A British House of Commons report as far back as 1837 said that Aboriginal people have "plain and sacred right" to their land. Only since 1976 has this right been recognized.

There is also a National Aboriginal Conference that acts to advise the government about the wishes of the Aboriginal people. The representatives of these organizations now travel all over the world to meet with other indigenous peoples.

Respect for Aboriginal beliefs and their way of life has grown. This beautiful bark painting shows the passage of the soul after death.

People vs. Profit

The business of the mining companies is to dig up minerals from the earth and sell them at a profit. This often causes great destruction to the land and environment and causes distress to the Aboriginal owners of the land. Their sacred places and objects are damaged and destroyed. The Aborigines of Noonkanbah in northwest Australia said in 1979 that this destruction "breaks our spirit as a people." They can no longer hunt and gather freely where mining companies operate.

Some Aboriginal communities do not want mining at all on their land. Others, like the *Pitjantjatjara,*

SITE OF SIGNIFICANCE

BEYOND THIS POINT LIES AN ABORIGINAL SITE OF A SACRED/DANGEROUS NATURE

UNDER SECTION 69 OF THE ABORIGINAL LAND RIGHTS (NORTHERN TERRITORY) ACT 1976

TRESPASS ON A SACRED SITE CARRIES A PENALTY OF

$1,000

ONE THOUSAND DOLLARS.

BY REQUEST OF TRADITIONAL OWNERS

Pitjantjatjara *elders hold a Land Council meeting.*

Above *Some legislation exists to stop destruction of Aboriginal sacred sites.*

negotiate with the mining companies and tell them where not to dig. More and more companies are willing to sit down with Aborigines and negotiate in this way. Others, however, still insist that Aborigines must not stand in the way of progress.

When the companies are allowed to mine, Aborigines negotiate for a percentage of the money made from the minerals. They also negotiate for compensation where their lives and land are disrupted. The communities use this money for things they need, things that most other Australians have, like housing and health and education facilities. Aborigines buy guns and trucks to hunt and gather food easily. Trucks are also useful in gathering the people together for ceremonial business. Radios keep the outstations in contact with each other or are used to call for a doctor when someone is unwell. Bores are sunk for water when the nearest well might be some 50 miles (80 kilometers) away.

The conflict between black and white Australians over the use of land began right back in 1788. In the past, the needs of the white community overrode the rights of the Aborigines. There are still many misunderstandings on both sides. The ownership of the land is very important for Aboriginal people. It is necessary for their cultural strength and for their independence. It rightfully belongs to them.

Mining in Australia has often been the cause of great destruction to Aboriginal land.

"Listen to Us!"

The Aboriginal culture — the ceremonies, songs, arts, dances, rituals, languages and Laws — means a lot to Aboriginal people. For some Aborigines, like the *Pitjantjatjara*, it is still strong. The people in the towns and cities are now wanting to learn more about their roots. This knowledge was all but destroyed when they were removed from their land. But the urge to learn about their culture and history is a powerful urge among young Aborigines.

An Aboriginal family from New South Wales in front of the Aboriginal flag.

Above Pitjantjatjara *women make their views known at a tribal meeting.*

Aboriginal schools, such as Yipirinya (in the Northern Territory), Yiyili (in Western Australia) and Murawina (in Sydney), teach children in both the Aboriginal and the European way. The whole community is often involved in the business of schooling. But there are still too few of these schools, designed especially for Aboriginal needs.

Aboriginal people are working together more and more all over Australia. The future looks brighter because of this growing strength.

This map shows those areas where Aborigines hold inalienable right to their land (April 1984).

More white people are supporting Aboriginal rights. The *Pitjantjatjara* Land Rights song calls to all the Australian people:

Listen to us,
Our country is very beautiful.
It is our grandfather's and our grandmother's country from a long time ago.
Listen to us.
It is the sacred ground of the Dreamtime.
Why do you never understand?
I always speak like this,
Don't take our country or we will die.
How can you buy my grandfather?

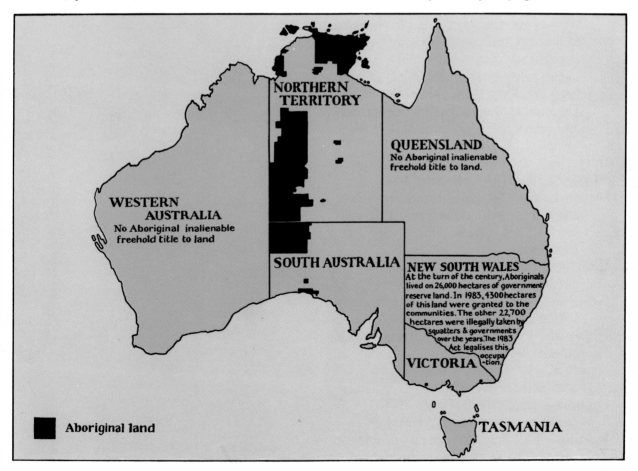

NORTHERN TERRITORY

QUEENSLAND
No Aboriginal inalienable freehold title to land.

WESTERN AUSTRALIA
No Aboriginal inalienable freehold title to land

SOUTH AUSTRALIA

NEW SOUTH WALES
At the turn of the century, Aboriginals lived on 26,000 hectares of government reserve land. In 1983, 4300 hectares of this land were granted to the communities. The other 22,700 hectares were illegally taken by squatters & governments over the years. The 1983 Act legalises this occupation.

VICTORIA

Aboriginal land

TASMANIA

Glossary

Anthropologist A person who studies human societies and customs.

Bush tucker Food collected in the outback.

Clan A group of people who claim descent from one of the Ancestral Beings. They had in common the same inherited Dreaming (usually an animal, plant or other natural thing).

Colonization The occupation of lands by a foreign people sometimes with the consent of the original owners but also, as in Australia, by force.

Country camps Not a holiday camp as we know it. If we understand "country" as meaning everything from home to place of birth, then we may begin to understand how important country camps are. People are more able to keep the Law, learn the stories of the Dreamtime, gather food to stay healthy and retain some independence in these camps.

Dilly bag A small bag made of braided grass, used for collecting food.

Dispossession To have something taken away from you. Aborigines had their land taken from them by the Europeans.

Discrimination Unfair treatment of a person, racial group or minority.

Genocide The practice of deliberately killing a particular people either because of their race, religion, color, culture or politics.

Heathen A person who does not acknowledge the God of Christianity.

Humpies Small, badly built shelters on fringe camps in which Aborigines live.

Kinship The way in which people in society are related to each other.

Aborigines were related through skin groups.

Referendum The submission of an important issue to the direct vote of the people.

Segregation The act of separating people.

Totem An object, animal or plant that symbolizes a clan or family and has ritual associations.

Tribe More accurately called a language group because they share the same language, and one set of customs, beliefs and ceremonies.

Tuberculosis A contagious disease of the lungs.

Glossary of Pitjantjatjara Words

Anangu The people.
Ili Wild fig, a commonly eaten food.
Kapi Water.
Kunka A young woman without children.
Malu Everyone knows the kangaroo!
Manta Land, ground or earth.
Milmilpa Sacred.
Minyma A married woman with two children.
Muni-muni A game using leaves as puppets.
Ngura Home, camp or country. The place to which a person belongs and which belongs to that person.
Pura Bush tomato.
Tjala The honey ant, delicious and highly prized.
Tjitji A child before initiation.
Tjitjitjuta Children.
Tjukurpa The Dreamtime or Dreaming. Also means the Law of the Dreamtime.
Wati An initiated man.

Books to read

Some of the books listed here may no longer be in print but should still be available in libraries.

An Aboriginal Family by Rollo Browne (Lerner, 1985).
Australia: The Land and its People by Elizabeth Cornelia (Silver, 1978).
We Live in Australia by Rennie Ellis (Watts, 1983).
Aborigines of Australia by Olga Hoyt (Lothrop, 1969).
Australia by Emilie U. Lepthien (Childrens Press, 1982).
Aborigines by Virginia Luling (Silver, 1979).
Ngari: The Hunter by Ronald Rose (Harcourt, 1968).

Acknowledgments

The illustrations in this book were supplied by the following:

Australian Information Service, London 21, 23 (top), 27 (bottom), 39 (top), 43; Australian Institute for Aboriginal Studies 28; Colorific (Penny Tweedie) 9 (bottom), 13 (bottom), 16, 18, 23 (bottom), 24 (bottom), 29 (bottom), 36 (bottom), 40; John Fairfax and Sons 36; Pamela Gill 29; Elaine Pelot Kitchener 35 (top and bottom), 40 (top); Eric Maddern *Frontispiece;* Axel Poignant 8, 9 (top), 10 (top), 11, 12, 14, 17, 19 (top), 20, 25, 26, 29 (top), 30, 31 (bottom), 33 (bottom), 41 (bottom); Penny Tweedie 10 (bottom), 13 (top), 19 (top), 22, 24 (top), 34, 37, 42 (bottom). The remaining illustrations are from the Wayland Picture Library. The maps on pages 7 and 45 were supplied by Andy Martin.

Index

Aborigines
  adaptation of 7, 35, 37
  attitudes 18, 19
  beliefs 20
  culture 7, 20, 22, 24, 35, 36, 37, 43, 44
  diet 28
  extended family 15
  homes 15, 40
  manhood 25
  origins 13, 16
  their future 45
  womanhood 25
Aboriginal Legal Services 40
Aboriginal Medical Services 40
Aboriginal Tent Embassy 39
Adelaide, Bishop of 30
Alcohol 32
Ancestral Beings 6, 8, 9, 12, 13, 16, 17, 18, 29
Aranda tribe 12
Australian government 33, 35, 37
  policies of 31, 34, 37, 40

Boomerang 19
British colonization 6, 14, 20, 27, 30, 31
British House of Commons report (1837) 41

Child mortality 36
Children 17, 19, 20, 21, 22, 24, 36
Christianity 30
Climate 15, 18
Cook, Captain James 26

Discrimination 38
Disease 28, 33, 36
Dreamtime religion 6, 7, 9, 10, 13, 25
  background 8
  Dreaming, the 6, 10, 11, 27, 32, 39
  Dreaming place 10, 17
  Dreaming tracks 8, 18
  Laws of 6, 11, 17, 19, 25
  sacred sites of 9, 16, 42
  songs of 19

Education 23, 24, 25, 26, 40, 43, 44
Equal Rights Campaigns 38, 39

Food 6, 15, 16, 18, 32
Fringe dwellers 36

Games 22

Health facilities 40, 43
Honey Ant Dreaming 10, 17
Hunting 19, 43

Identity 37

Kinship system 20
  rules 21, 22

Land Councils 41
Land Rights Act (1976) 39
Languages 7, 14, 22, 23, 35, 44

Malnutrition 36
Marriage 21, 32
Mineral resources 43
Missionaries 30, 31, 33
Mixed-race children 31

National Aboriginal Conference 41
National Federation of Land Councils 41

Pitjantjatjara tribe 7, 14, 18, 42, 44, 45

Racism 37
Religion 6, 30, 36
Reserves 32, 33, 34, 38
Right to vote 38

Schools 44
Self-determination 40, 43
Skin names 21

Totem 10, 29
Tribal lands 16, 33, 38

White Australians 16, 32

White Society 20, 30, 32, 33, 35, 36, 37, 38
World War, Second 34